# Bang the

Stan Cullimore, Rosalind Kerven
and Fiona Macdonald

## Contents

**The Steel Band**
*by Stan Cullimore* ........................................................ 2

**Drums and other Percussion Instruments**
*by Fiona Macdonald* .................................................. 16

**The Singing Drum**
*by Rosalind Kerven* ................................................... 24

**Glossary** ................................................................. 32

# The Steel Band

Stan Cullimore

Mum popped her head round the door to Abbie's bedroom.

"Abbie, what are you doing?" she asked.

Abbie was sitting reading at her desk listening to the radio and tapping her fingers in time to the music. She saw her mother and stopped drumming on the desk. "Just finishing my homework," she replied.

Mum smiled. "I'm going out to a band **rehearsal**. I thought that perhaps you would like to come along and watch."

Abbie jumped up. "Yes, please."

"I thought you'd say that," said Mum.

Half an hour later Abbie and her mother were outside the room where the band rehearsed.

"Do you think Mr See will let me have a go on any of the steel drums tonight?" asked Abbie.

"I expect so," replied Mum.

Abbie pushed open the door and went inside. All around the room people were getting their instruments ready. A lady was taking her saxophone out of its case. A man with a trumpet was warming up his lips by blowing a few notes. A boy sitting at a drum kit was softly beating out a **rhythm**.

Abbie looked around until she saw a familiar face. "Mr See," she cried.

Mr See waved and gave Abbie a big smile.

"Hello there my sweet," he said.

The middle of the room was filled with over a dozen steel drums. They were made from the tops of large, metal oil drums, standing on legs. The drum tops had been hammered into a strange pattern of shapes. Each shape had been tuned to play a single note when hit with a beater. If you knew which shape to beat, you could play a tune on the drums.

Mr See took a pair of beaters out of a bag on the floor. He gave the beaters to Abbie.

"Go on," he said, "have a go!"

Abbie took the beaters and stepped up to a steel drum. She began to tap out a tune. Bing, bong, bang, bing, bong, bang!

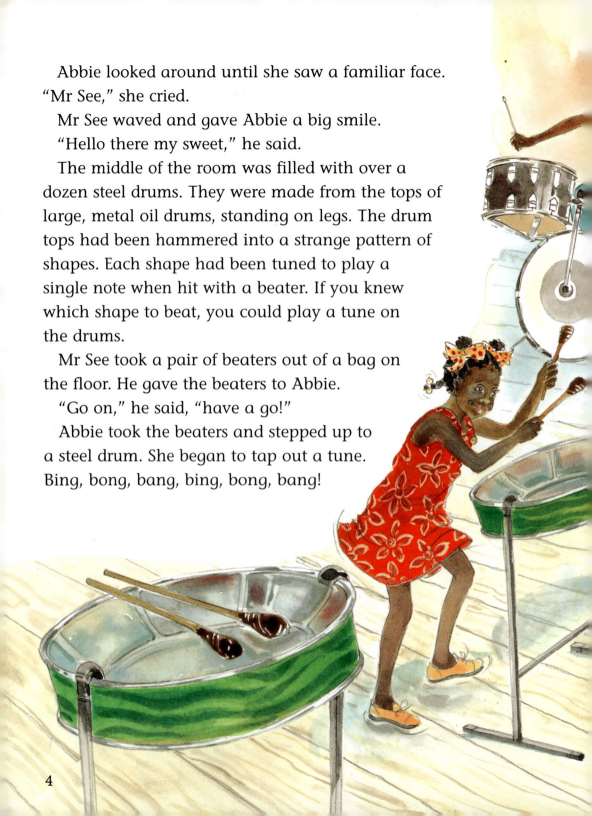

The sound of the steel drum filled the room. Abbie didn't understand how to play the different notes so she used the three nearest shapes on the drum. As she played she began to dance. She just loved the feel of the rhythm floating through the air and into her feet.

The boy on the drum kit began to play along in time to the rhythm of Abbie's steel drum.

After a few moments Mr See came over to Abbie. He grinned down at her.

"Young lady, you are a natural musician. Rhythm is in your soul."

"When I'm older I'm going to play in a steel band," said Abbie.

"I'm sure you'll be very good at it," Mr See nodded.

He clapped his hands together. "Now, if everyone is ready, I think we should start our rehearsal. We have to be ready for the carnival on Saturday."

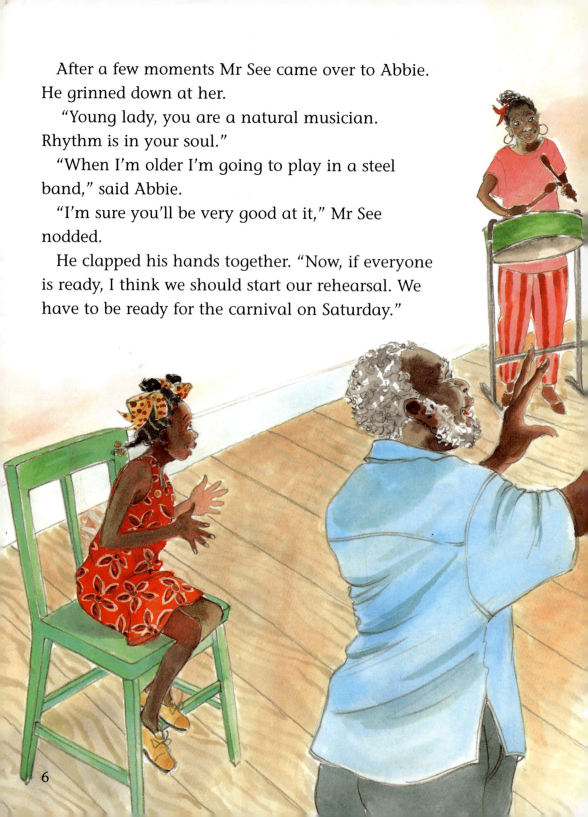

For the next hour the band went through the songs they were going to play at the carnival. Abbie loved every minute of it. She hummed along with the tunes that the steel drums played. She tapped her feet in time to the drums' loud beat. When the man with the trumpet stood up to play a **duet** with the lady on the saxophone, Abbie squealed with delight. All too soon it was time for the band to pack up and go home.

"The duet between the saxophone and the trumpet is great," Mr See said, shaking his head. "But we need something special to finish it off at the end."

Just as Abbie and her mother were about to leave the hall, Mr See came over to them. He was holding a large brown bag.

"Tell me, Abbie," he said, "do you really want to play in a steel band when you are older?"

Abbie leapt up into the air. "YES, please!" she shouted.

Mr See smiled to himself. "Well, you don't really have to be grown up to play in our band. You can start whenever you want to."

He put the large brown bag down on the floor. "Now, let me see, what have I got in here?"

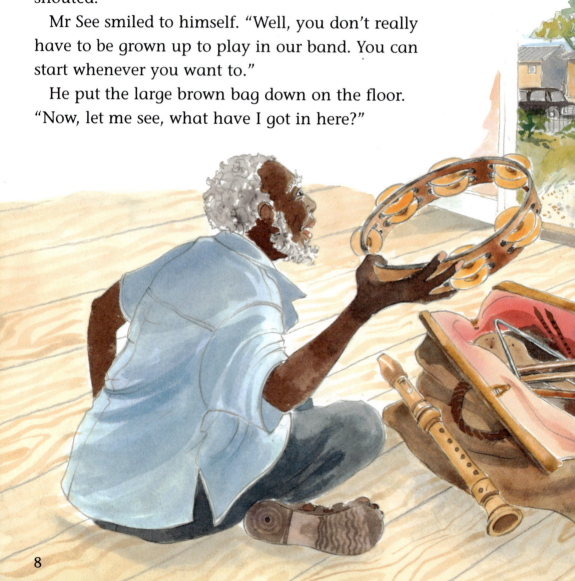

Mr See opened the large brown bag.

"Wow," gasped Abbie. She had never seen so many strange-looking instruments before in her life.

Mr See pulled out a recorder. "Have you ever played one of these?" he asked.

Abbie shook her head. "No."

Mr See pulled out a tambourine. "How about one of these?"

Abbie shook her head again.

Mr See looked thoughtful.

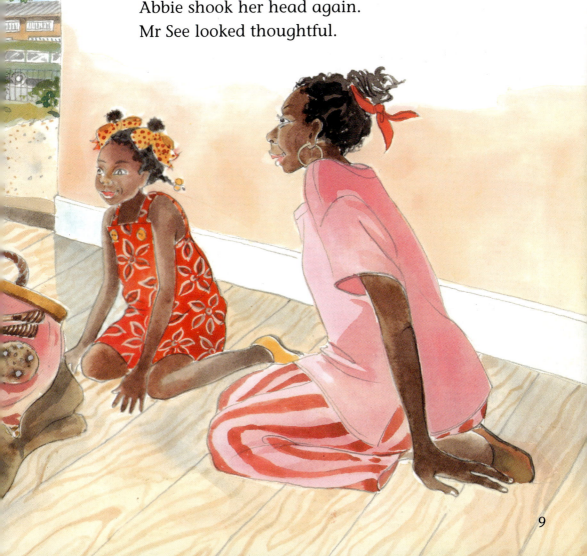

The next thing Mr See pulled out was a pair of maracas.

Abbie nodded. "I've played those at school. They make a sort of rattling noise when you shake them."

She picked them up and gave them both a shake to try them out. She soon managed to get a rhythm going as she danced from foot to foot.

Mr See smiled. "That's right. Would you like to take them home and practise with them?"

"Yes, please!" replied Abbie.

"Bring them along to the rehearsal on Friday," added Mr See, "and if you're any good – I might just let you join the band!"

A few days later Abbie and her mother were back in the rehearsal room. It was the last rehearsal before the carnival and everyone was eager to start.

"Abbie, you can come over here and stand by me," said Mr See. "I want to see if you can shake your maracas in time to the music."

For the next hour the band played through their songs. The steel drums played the melody, the drum kept the beat, and Abbie shook her maracas as hard as she could.

At long last, Mr See held up his hand.

"OK, that's enough," he said. "The duet still needs something to finish it off – but I don't know what."

The band began to pack away their instruments.

"See you all in the park at ten tomorrow morning," said Mr See.

He went over to Abbie. "So, Abbie, are you glad you have joined our band?"

Abbie pulled a face, "No, not really," she replied.

Mr See looked puzzled. "Why not?" he asked.

Abbie looked down at the maracas in her hand. "These are too quiet. I couldn't hear them above the rest of the band. There's no point in being in the band if no one can hear me," she explained.

Mr See looked thoughtful. "I see," he said.

He took the maracas from Abbie. He shook them as hard as he could. Then he pulled a face.

"I see what you mean," he said. "They are a bit quiet."

Mr See knelt down on the floor so that he could look right into Abbie's eyes. "You've just given me an idea. There is something else you could play. But I have to warn you. These are the loudest instruments in the whole band."

"Really?" asked Abbie. "What are they?"

Mr See tapped the side of his nose.

"Come along tomorrow morning and I'll show you," he said.

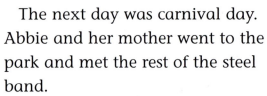

The next day was carnival day. Abbie and her mother went to the park and met the rest of the steel band.

"OK, everyone! Set up here," shouted Mr See. "We start our performance in twenty minutes."

He turned to Abbie. "Ready?" he asked.

Abbie nodded.

Mr See opened his bag and took out two large round objects. He handed them to Abbie. "Do you know what these are?" he asked.

"Yes!" Abbie replied.

"Good! Then don't let them touch each other until I tell you. Otherwise you'll deafen everyone," Mr See explained.

By half past ten a large crowd had gathered to listen to the band. They began to play. The audience and musicians all enjoyed themselves. At last it was time for the final song. It was the song where the saxophone and trumpet played their duet.

"Get ready, Abbie," whispered Mr See.

Abbie waited. The duet began. It was beautiful. The sound filled the air. As the duet reached its **crescendo**, Mr See turned to Abbie.

"NOW!"

Abbie waited until the last notes drifted up to the sky. Then she lifted the cymbals she was holding. She brought them CRASHING together.

The crowd burst into applause.

Mr See winked at Abbie. "Now that's what I call a real finish!" he whispered.

# DRUMS
### and other Percussion Instruments

Fiona Macdonald

**What are percussion instruments?**
Musical instruments that produce a sound when they are hit, shaken or scraped, are called **percussion instruments**. They get their name from the way they are played. "Percussion" means "by hitting".

There are hundreds of different percussion instruments, and they all make different sounds – from soft, gentle chimes to loud crashes, booms and rumbles. The sound each one makes depends on what it is made from, how it is hit, and whether it is solid or hollow. Large instruments are usually louder than small ones.

Some percussion instruments are tuned. They produce a particular range of low to high notes, called the **pitch**. Untuned percussion instruments produce sounds with no fixed pitch at all.

Percussion instruments are sometimes played alone, but they are usually played as part of an **orchestra**, band or group. They provide the regular beat or **rhythm** for the other instruments to follow. Percussion instruments are played all around the world.

17

**How do we hear percussion instruments?**
When players hit or shake a percussion instrument, it produces **sound-waves** that travel through the air. Each instrument produces different sound-waves, depending on how quickly or slowly it **vibrates**.

The sound-waves that a tuned percussion instrument makes are **regular**. The sound-waves that an untuned percussion instrument makes are **irregular**.

When these sound-waves reach our ears, tiny bones inside them start vibrating at the same speed as the instrument we are listening to. Special cells turn these vibrations into electrical signals, and nerves carry these signals to our brains. When our brains receive the signals, they "read" them – and we hear music!

Our brains soon learn to recognize the different sounds made by different instruments. This means we can tell which instrument is being played without having to see it. To test this for yourself, shut your eyes and ask a friend to play two different percussion instruments. Can you recognize each one by the sound it makes?

# A–Z of percussion instruments

## Afuche to Cymbals

### Afuche (or Cabasa)
- from South America
- gourd covered with beads, or made from wood and metal
- scraping sound when turned round and round
- untuned
- played in bands

### Castanets
- from Spain
- wood
- clapping sound when shaken
- untuned
- played by dancers, and in orchestras

### Chime bars
- from many countries
- metal bars attached to holders
- ringing sound when hit with a hammer
- tuned
- played in bands

### Bells
- from many countries
- metal
- ringing chimes when hit from outside with a hammer, or from inside by a "tongue" or clapper
- tuned
- often played in religious ceremonies

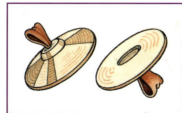

### Cymbals
- from Turkey
- metal
- loud crashing sound when banged together, and a softer noise when gently rubbed or hit with a stick
- untuned
- played in orchestras and bands

19

## D for Drum

Drums come from many countries. They were the first musical instruments to be invented, thousands of years ago. They are made of wood, metal or clay and topped with either animal skins or plastic. They make rattling, tapping, knocking or booming sounds.

In the past, drums were used to send signals or warnings. Today, they are played in orchestras, rock groups and bands. Their beat makes people want to dance. They are also used by soldiers. The regular beat helps them to march in step. Drums can be tuned or untuned. Here are some of them:

### Bass drum
- from Europe
- metal frame, animal-skin top with sheepskin-topped drumsticks
- deep, booming sound
- untuned

### Bodhran
- from Ireland
- wooden frame, animal-skin top, wooden beater
- booming sound
- untuned

### Bongos
- from Africa and South America
- wooden frame, animal-skin top
- brisk, tapping sound played with the hands
- tuned

### Side drum or snare drum
- from Europe
- metal frame, animal-skin top, metal strings or snares with wooden drumsticks
- sharp, rattling sound
- untuned

### Tabla
- from India
- pottery frame or wooden frame, animal-skin top
- clear, hollow sound, played with the fingers
- untuned

### Steel drums or pans
- from the Caribbean
- metal frame, shaped metal drum-head, tapped with metal hammers
- ringing, humming sound
- tuned

### Tambourine
- from Turkey
- wooden frame, animal-skin or plastic top with metal bells
- rattling, jingling sound played by shaking and tapping
- untuned

### Timpani or kettledrums
- from the Middle East
- metal frame, animal-skin top, wooden drumsticks
- loud, strong sound
- tuned

21

# Gamelan to Xylophone

### Gamelan
- from Java, Indonesia
- made of metal
- ringing, rippling sound
- tuned
- Not a single instrument, but an orchestra of percussion instruments, including gongs and xylophones. Played at concerts and performances with singers and dancers.

### Ganza
- from South America
- metal tubes filled with metal pellets or small stones
- whooshing sound when shaken
- untuned
- played in bands

### Glockenspiel
- from Germany
- metal bars on a wooden base
- chiming sound when hit with small hard hammers
- tuned
- played in orchestras

### Gong
- from China and Central Asia
- metal
- booming, echoing sound when hit with a large soft hammer
- untuned
- In the past, used to send signals and make announcements, now played in orchestras

## Triangle
- from Europe
- steel rod, bent into triangle shape
- tinkling sound when hit with a metal beater
- untuned
- played in bands and orchestras

## Guiro
- from South America
- dried gourd with a rough surface, or made from wood
- produces a rasping sound when scraped with a stick
- untuned
- played in bands

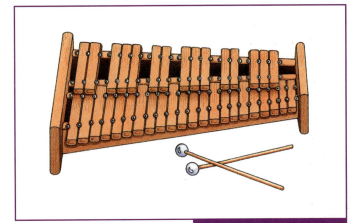

## Xylophone
- from Africa
- wooden bars on a metal frame
- bright, ringing sound when hit with hammers
- tuned
- played in bands and orchestras

## Maracas
- from South America
- round gourds filled with small stones, or from plastic
- rattling sound when shaken
- untuned
- played in bands

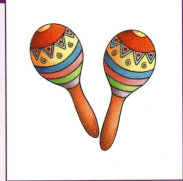

23

# THE SINGING DRUM

## A Swahili Folk tale from East Africa

Rosalind Kerven

Once, a girl went out with her friends to play on the beach. There she found a beautiful white shell, hidden in the sand. She put it on a rock to keep it safe, and ran off again to play.

At sunset the children went home. But on the way, the girl suddenly remembered the shell. She begged her friends to come back with her and fetch it, but none of them would. So she ran back to the beach by herself.

It was getting quite dark by now and the beach was full of shadows. The girl was really afraid.

She ran from rock to rock, looking for the shell. As she ran, she sang a song to make herself feel brave:

> "Ooh la-la, ooh la-la,
> Lovely seashell,
> Ooh la-la, ooh la-la,
> Lovely seashell…"

Suddenly, she saw it, gleaming white as the moon against the night. But something else was there too, sitting on the rock beside it. It was a nasty, twisted, wicked goblin.

The girl screamed and tried to back away.

"Don't be afraid of me, little girl," hissed the goblin. "Come closer. Let me hear your song again." He licked his lips. "If you sing it nicely, I might give you back your shell."

The girl didn't know what to do. She stood there trembling. At last, in a very low voice she sang:

"Ooh la-la, ooh la-la,
Lovely seashell,
Ooh la…"

"I can't hear you," snapped the goblin. "Come right up to me."

Then suddenly he leaped off the rock and grabbed her arm. He pushed her into a big wooden drum, and banged its lid tightly shut!

"Hah!" hissed the goblin, "now you're my prisoner and I can make you sing whenever I want!"

He kicked the drum up the beach and rolled it along the road. Inside it, the poor girl tumbled and bumped about. Soon she was bruised and aching all over.

But at long last, the drum stopped. The goblin put his face by a crack in the wood and whispered:

"Soon we will come to a village. When I play the drum, you must sing that pretty song. If you do, I shall feed you. But if you don't, I'll throw you to the lions!"

By the time they reached the village, it was morning. The goblin pushed the drum to the centre of the market place.

"Hey, everybody," he shouted. "Come and hear my magic singing drum!"

All the people turned to stare at him. The goblin pulled a stick from his belt and began to beat the drum.

Inside it, the frightened girl choked back her tears and sang:

"Ooh la-la, ooh la-la,
Lovely seashell."

The people were amazed. "However does that strange little fellow make the singing drum work?" they asked.

"It's my secret magic," said the goblin. "Now you've heard it, you've got to pay me. Give me food!"

And he tried to beat the villagers with his drumstick until they ran off and fetched him a huge dish of roast chicken.

The goblin gobbled it up greedily. Then he pushed a few leftover scraps into the drum for the girl.

Later, he pushed the drum to the next village. And so they went on, travelling around everywhere with the "singing drum".

Soon they became very famous. No one ever guessed the goblin's wicked secret.

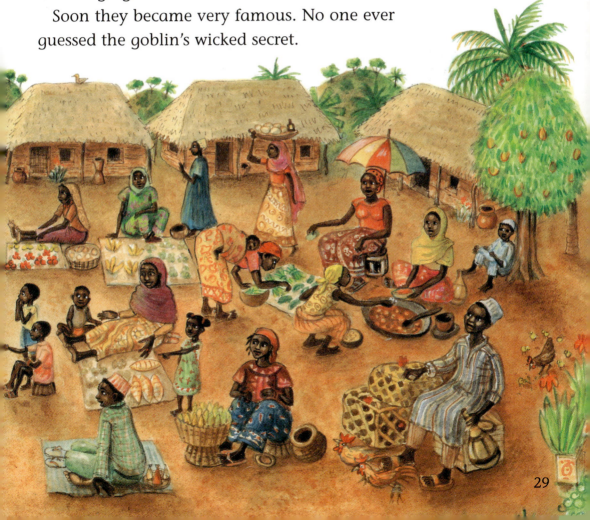

29

One day, they came to the girl's own village. When everyone hurried out to hear the famous singing drum, the girl's own mother and father were there too. They looked so sad without their daughter.

Well, as soon as the goblin beat the drum and the singing started, the father cried:

"Listen to that voice! That sounds just like our daughter, singing inside the drum!"

The mother pulled him away quickly. "Ssshh!" she whispered. "I'm sure you're right. But be careful. We'll have to trick the goblin if we're going to rescue her alive. Listen, I know what to do."

When the goblin had finished his show, the girl's father went to him and said,

"My friend, would you like a drink before you go?"

"Give me some beer," said the goblin, rudely.

So the father fetched an enormous jar of frothy beer. The goblin gulped it all down in no time. Then he swayed and wobbled. He was drunk! He fell down into a deep sleep.

Quickly, the mother and father ran to his drum and forced open the lid. Out jumped the girl, safe and sound, straight into their arms.

And you can imagine how glad they were to see each other!

# Glossary

**crescendo**  A crescendo is a gradual increase in loudness.

**duet**  A duet is a piece of music performed by two players or singers.

**irregular**  Something that is irregular is uneven.

**orchestra**  An orchestra is a large group of people playing various musical instruments together.

**percussion instruments**  These are musical instruments that are played by hitting or shaking them.

**pitch**  The pitch of a sound is its highness or lowness.

**regular**  Something that is regular is even.

**rehearsal**  Musicians and actors have to practice together before they perform to an audience. This practice session is called a rehearsal.

**rhythm**  A rhythm is a regular pattern of beats, sounds or movements.

**sound-waves**  Sound travels through the air in waves, like ripples on a pond.

**vibrate**  Something that vibrates is moving to and fro very quickly. Sounds are vibrations in the air.